Top Tunes for Teaching

977 Song Titles and Practical Tools for Choosing the Right Music Every Time

Eric Jensen

Top Tunes for Teaching

977 Song Titles and Practical Tools for Choosing the Right Music Every Time

©2005 Eric Jensen
Cover design: Tracy Linares
Text design: Jan Fenner
Editing: Karen Miller

The Brain Store
4202 Sorrento Valley Blvd., Ste. B • San Diego, CA 92121
phone: (800) 325-4769, (858) 546-7555 • fax: (858) 546-7560
www.thebrainstore.com • email: info@thebrainstore.com

Printed in the United States of America
Published by The Brain Store
San Diego, CA, USA

ISBN #1-890460-43-5

Acknowledgements

Many others contributed directly and indirectly with song ideas. Those contributors include Arturo Flores, Karen Miller, Tracy Linares, and Rich Allen. I am very appreciative and deeply indebted for their suggestions.

Table of Contents

Introduction

"Your music is SO good! Where'd you find it?" Teachers and trainers ask me this every single time I present. For years, I've collected great music, perfect for learning that I now want to share with other educational professionals.

The purpose of this book is to provide support for teachers and trainers who love to use music in the classroom but are not sure of how or when or which piece of music fits a situation. *Top Tunes for Teaching* is mostly a book of lists of tunes and artists, so I hope it's easy to use. There are dozens of lists and hundreds of songs in this book, some of which you may not be familiar with. Be sure to screen songs you don't know before playing them in front of a group—that way you can avoid surprises like extremely long introductions or PG-13 lyrics in front of a K–3 class!

This book is a storehouse of practical tidbits sprinkled throughout with scientific research and rationale. It was really fun for me to write and I hope it is just as much fun for you to read and use. If you have any favorite selections or suggestions you think should be in the next edition, please e-mail them to me at eric@jlcbrain.com—I'd love your input.

Have fun!

Eric Jensen

Using This Book

Why Music Matters

How to Use Music in the Classroom

Music for Specific Purposes

10 Great Reasons to Use Music

You probably already know all the good reasons for using music while you teach, but have you ever tried to articulate them to others? Here is a good list of reasons why music benefits learning.

1. *Increase social contact.* Music encourages social contact by putting people into a positive, relaxed mental state. Louder music can bring others close together if only so they can hear each other better! Familiar, fun music puts groups in a social mood.

2. *Prime students for learning.* Prepare learners for upcoming tasks by selecting music to put them in a particular emotional state or by playing a song with content-applicable lyrics (there really are songs about science, geography, math, English, and P. E.).

3. *Entrain emotional states of mind.* When everyone in the audience hears the same piece of music over time, they often get into the same emotional state, mental rhythm, and frame of mind. Music creates a harmonic beacon for our bodies to follow.

4. *Deliver key messages.* Sometimes music can send a message to your students better than you can. Certain songs can do that well; browse the lists of songs in this book for ideas and recommendations.

5. *Provide a background for physical movement.* Up-tempo music playing in the background prompts learners to move faster. When you want them to get up and perform a physical task, play a song from the *18 Pumped-Up, High-Energy Jams* or *10 More Upbeat Energizers* lists on pages 36 and 43.

6. *Evoke specific memories.* Certain songs may remind listeners of what they were doing when they first heard that song. Other songs may invite the listener to evoke a new memory not previously associated with that song. Experiment with both.

7. *Energize a group.* Fast music, or music with 100 to 140 beats per minute (BPM), is both stressful and energizing. Use it as a strategic tool to get students up on their feet and moving or busily working to meet a deadline. (See *3 Ways to Pace Instruction with Beats per Minute* on page 14.)

8. *Establish an auditory backdrop.* Music playing in the background can provide a stable, predictable backdrop to the day's events. The next time you watch a movie, pay attention to how often music is played in the background. The music you choose should match and enhance the direction of the day, not overwhelm it. Instrumental music with 55 to 70 BPM works best for this purpose.

9. *Calm the mind and body.* Slow-paced music practically forces the body and mind to slow down to its tempo. Play music at 40 to 55 BPM and expect miracles! Two lists of relaxing music, *15 Soothing, Inspiring Tunes* and *17 Albums to Calm the Mind and Soothe the Body*, appear on pages 27 and 46.

10. *Heal.* There is some scientific evidence that music, when used in certain ways, reduces stress and strengthens the immune system.

Blood, D. J. & Ferriss, S. J. (1993, Feb). Effects of background music on anxiety, satisfaction with communication, and productivity. *Psychological Reports*, 72(1), 171–7.

McCraty, R., Atkinson, M., Rein, G., & Watkins, A. D. (1996). Music enhances the effect of positive emotional state on salivary IgA. *Stress Medicine*, 12(3), 167–75.

Bartlett, D., Kaufman, D., & Smeltekop, R. (1993). The effects of music listening and perceived sensory experiences on the immune system as measured by interleukin-1 and cortisol. *Journal of Music Therapy*, 30(4), 194–209.

Rider, M. & Achterberg, J. (1989). Effect of music-assisted imagery on neutrophils and lymphocytes. *Biofeedback and Self-Regulation*, 14(3), 247–57.

Lane, D. (1991). The effect of a single music therapy session on hospitalized children as measured by salivary immunoglobin A, speech pause time, and a patient opinion Likert scale. *Dissertation Abstracts International*, 52(7-B), 3522.

7 Reasons Why Music Should Be Part of Every Curriculum

1. *Music is assessable.* Although it's relatively difficult to assess the musical arts, it can and has been done. There is much value in creating strong assessment procedures that recognize the characteristics and limitations inherent in teaching and learning the musical arts. It is also more fun for students to study the musical arts on a credit/no credit basis.

2. *Music curriculum is brain-based.* Just as there are language centers in the brain, there are also areas that respond specifically to music. The musical arts not only engage many areas of the brain, they have multiple and far-reaching effects on the mind. We really can say that music has a biological basis.

3. *Music is culturally necessary.* Music promotes social skills that enhance a person's awareness of others and tolerance for differences. It also promotes unity and harmony. It enhances cognitive and perceptual skills and serves as a vehicle for cultural identity and free expression.

4. *Music curriculum has no significant downside.* There are no known cases of a music curriculum, either integrated or modular, being faulted for lowering student test scores or reducing graduation rates. Some types of music, however (like heavy metal and rap), are correlated with aggressive and dysfunctional behaviors.

5. *Music is inclusive.* Music breaks down barriers between races, religions, cultures, geographic distinctions, and socioeconomic strata. The Suzuki method (a strategy for teaching music to young children by listening, absorbing, and copying a musician) demonstrates that with the proper instruction, almost everyone can learn to play music. The musical arts have the capacity to engage us all.

6. *Music has a survival value.* The musical arts help define, support, and transmit culture from one generation to the next. Because music transmits important societal values, it facilitates the creation of strong and large communities.

7. *Music is wide-ranging.* The musical arts encompass a wide range of talents and skills: performance music, music listening, song writing, arranging, analysis, singing, improvisation, and conducting. Taken as a whole, the musical arts are deep in substance and suitable for everyone.

Gardstrom, S. C. (1999). Music exposure and criminal behavior: Perceptions of juvenile offenders. *Journal of Music Therapy*, 36(3), 207–21.

Scheel, K. R. & Westefeld, J. S. (1999). Heavy metal music and adolescent suicidality: An empirical investigation. *Adolescence*, 34(134), 253–73.

11 All-Time Favorite Follow-Along Activity Songs

There are many "follow-along" songs that you can sing to and move to. The songs on this list are classics—your audience will happily jump in and join the fun.

1. Selections from *Tony Chestnut & Fun Time Action Songs* (available from The Learning Station)

2. *Hokey Pokey* (traditional)

3. *Shake Your Brain* (Red Grammer)

4. *Jump Down, Spin Around* (Harry Belafonte)

5. *YMCA* (Village People)

6. *Macarena* (Los Del Mar)

7. The "Chicken Dance," or *Der Ententanz* (Werner Thomas)

8. *Monkey in the Middle* (on the CD, *Physical Ed*, from The Learning Station)

9. *Side Slide* (also on the CD, *Physical Ed*, from The Learning Station)

10. *Twelve Days of Gym Class* (also on the CD, *Physical Ed*, from The Learning Station)

11. *Can You Keep Your Balance?* (also on the CD, *Physical Ed*, from The Learning Station)

11 Ways Music Positively Affects the Brain and Body

Although the research demonstrates that not all types music benefit every brain or body, one thing is clear: Music has beneficial effects.

Music:

1. Increases muscular energy

2. Aids in the release of emotions

3. Influences heartbeat

4. Alters overall metabolism

5. Reduces the sensation of pain

6. Speeds healing and recovery in surgery patients

7. Counters fatigue

8. Changes brain chemistry

9. Improves mood

10. Stimulates creativity, sensitivity, and thinking

11. Relieves worry and stress

9 Facts about the Original Mozart Study

Frances Rauscher, Gordon Shaw, and lab assistant Katherine Ky conducted the original Mozart study in February, 1993 in Irvine, California. The experiment involved thirty-six college students who listened to either a Mozart composition (K448), a tape of relaxation instructions, or silence. After ten minutes of listening, they took a Stanford-Binet IQ test. The Mozart group performed significantly better on the task that required spatial abstract reasoning. This study was the first ever to show a causal relationship between listening to music and cognition. Since the original study, some researchers have been able to replicate and extend the findings; others have not.

This study showed that:

1. Listening to music causally changes cognitive processing.

2. Changes can begin after just ten minutes of listening to music.

3. Not all music has this the effect on cognitive processes.

It did not show that:

4. Listening to music makes you smarter.

5. The cognitive effects are triggered only by listening to Mozart compositions.

6. The cognitive effects are lasting.

You should know that:

7. This is a landmark study.

8. Many other studies (but not all) have replicated the results.

9. Highly rhythmic music will improve spatial abstract reasoning better than Mozart compositions.

Rauscher, F. H., Shaw, G. L., & Ky, K. N. (1993, Oct). Music and spatial task performance. *Nature*, 365(6447), 611.

15 "Can't Miss" Country Songs

There are many more "can't miss" country songs than the ones listed below—
these are just my favorites.

1. *I Walk the Line* (Johnny Cash)

2. *Cowboy, Take Me Away* (Dixie Chicks)

3. *Forever and for Always* (Shania Twain)

4. *You're Still the One* (Shania Twain)

5. *Breathe* (Faith Hill)

6. *On the Road Again* (Willie Nelson)

7. *I Wanna Talk about Me* (Toby Keith)

8. *Three Wooden Crosses* (Randy Travis)

9. *It's Five o'Clock Somewhere* (Alan Jackson)

10. *The Dance* (Garth Brooks)

11. *A Little Bit of Love (Goes a Long, Long Way)* (Wynonna Judd)

12. *Not a Moment Too Soon* (Tim McGraw)

13. *Rocky Mountain High* (John Denver)

14. *Crazy Little Thing Called Love* (Dwight Yoakum)

15. *The Fireman* (George Strait)

Songs to Rewrite as Part of a Lesson

1. *Happy Birthday to You*

2. *Jingle Bells*

3. *Old MacDonald Had a Farm*

4. *Row, Row, Row Your Boat*

5. *Twinkle, Twinkle Little Star*

6. *Rock Around the Clock* (Bill Haley and His Comets)

7. *The Twelve Days of Christmas*

Why rewrite a song as part of a lesson?

"Music acts as a premium signal carrier, whose rhythms, patterns, contrasts, and varying tonalities encode any new information" (Webb & Webb, 1990). Have you noticed how easily children pick up the word to new songs? The melody helps them remember the lyrics. Think of how easy it is for most children to learn the alphabet—they absorb the letters and their order to the tune of *Twinkle, Twinkle Little Star*, a melody they've been hearing over and over since infancy. When it's time to learn the alphabet, children "glue" the letters to the familiar tune. People do this so unconsciously that most of us don't even realize the alphabet song and *Twinkle, Twinkle Little Star* have the same melody. (And many of us probably still think of the tune in our heads when we try to remember if P or Q comes first!)

How do you incorporate rewriting songs into your lesson?

Have participants brainstorm and record key words or ideas from your presentation. Once they've spent time generating a good, long list, have them narrow it down to about ten items. Afterwards, ask them to brainstorm and record a list of commonly known songs that everyone knows the words to (but don't tell them why or what you plan to do with the two lists). The song lists usually consist of camp songs, nursery rhymes, folk tunes, and the like; seven are listed above if you need to make suggestions to get participants started.

After a few minutes of brainstorming, ask participant groups to vote for their favorite song on their list and rewrite the words, using the ten key terms from the other brainstorming list. For example, a third grade science class might come up with the lyrics, "Old MacDonald had a sun. E-I-E-I-O. And around this sun nine planets spun, E-I-E-I-O. With a Mercury here…," et cetera. Although I never require people to perform their songs for everybody, this activity is so fun that groups rarely refuse. (If you want, have each team write their lyrics on an overhead transparency so the entire class can sing along.)

Webb, D. & Webb, T. (1990). *Accelerated Learning with Music.* Norcross, GA: Accelerated Learning Systems.

5 Most Important Factors for Choosing What Music to Play

How do you decide which piece of music to play or which song will fit the moment? Before selecting any music, consider these five criteria. You may not find the perfect song for what you want (that comes with experience) but this process will help you find a good one.

1. What **emotional state** does this music evoke? (How do the beat, words, and melody make you feel?)

2. At what **volume** (low, medium, or high) do you want to play music?

3. What kind of **instrumentation** do you want? (Are you looking for solo vocals, a chorus, a solo instrument, an orchestra, big band, rock band, or electronic music?)

4. What **generation** are you trying to reach? (Did your audience grow up in the 1960s, 1970s, 1980s, or 1990s?)

5. What **culture** are you trying to reach? (Will your audience enjoy urban, country, hip-hop, bluegrass, alternative rock, folk music, or world beat?)

20 Upbeat Dance Songs from the 1980s

Great dance tunes open with a catchy, memorable beat that puts you in the mood immediately. When you listen to these songs, pay attention to the first thirty seconds. Believe it or not, but sometimes I use just the introduction to a song to get the effect I want, and then fade out the rest.

1. *Tonight She Comes* (The Cars)

2. *Hungry Like the Wolf* (Duran Duran)

3. *Every Little Thing She Does Is Magic* (The Police)

4. *Turning Japanese* (The Vapors)

5. *Brand New Lover* (Dead or Alive)

6. *Dancing in the Dark* (Bruce Springsteen)

7. *Wake Me Up before You Go-Go* (Wham!)

8. *She Bop* (Cyndi Lauper)

9. *Heart of Glass* (Blondie)

10. *You Spin Me Round* (Dead or Alive)

11. *Take On Me* (a-Ha)

12. *Don't Get Me Wrong* (The Pretenders)

13. *Walking on Sunshine* (Katrina and the Waves)

14. *Shake Your Love* (Debbie Gibson)

15. *Hungry Eyes* (Eric Carmen)

16. *Walk like an Egyptian* (The Bangles)

17. *Mony Mony* (Billy Idol)

18. *Girls on Film* (Duran Duran)

19. *Enola Gay* (OMD)

20. *Down Under* (Men at Work)

Things about the Music You Choose that Concern Listeners

You know what you want and how and why you choose the music you play. But have you ever thought about this process from a listener's point of view? Here are the things your students care about the most regarding music in the classroom:

1. *Familiarity*. How well do learners already know the music?

2. *Beat*. Does the tune have an identifiable, acceptable rhythm?

3. *Musical Atmosphere*. Is the music upbeat or a downer?

4. *Choice*. Are listeners given any choice about the music you play?

5. *Prior Experience*. Have learners had good or bad experiences with music in the classroom or with that particular selection?

6. *Catchy*. Are the melody and lyrics easy to remember and fun to hear?

7. *Peers*. How do their peers regard the music you play?

2 Other Important Considerations

8. *Set-Up*. Do you introduce the music apologetically or with enthusiasm?

9. *Location*. Where is the source of the music? Is it going to be too loud for some people who sit nearby?

20 Positive Ways Music Affects You and Your Audience

If there is something you want the audience to do, there is a piece of music that will inspire them to do it.

Music:

1. Activates the thinking portion of the brain

2. Adds an element of fun and novelty to a lesson

3. Appeals to the cultural values of a group

4. Arouses the brain and body

5. Builds rapport and encourages bonding

6. Calms down over-energetic students

7. Changes the mood of a classroom

8. Collects and brings whole groups together

9. Comforts the soul during painful times

10. Creates sound curtains to isolate classes or groups from distracting noise

11. Embeds the learning faster and on a deeper level (think of the alphabet song)

12. Energizes a group

13. Harmonizes a group when things get edgy

14. Helps build rapport within a group

15. Increases attentiveness and concentration

16. Provides relaxation after negative stress or discouragement

17. Boosts levels of productive stress and reduces discouragement

18. Spurs a group into action

19. Gives the presenter or teacher a moment's rest from "performing"

20. Triggers emotional responses

25 Canciones Fantásticas

If you haven't broadened your musical sphere to include artists and songs from Latin America, you are missing out. This music is catchy, energized, smooth, and romantic at times—you'll have to hear it to believe it. The songs on this list will whet your appetite for more.

1. *Dreaming of You* (Selena)

2. *Gavilán o Paloma* (José José)

3. *Un Fin de Semana* (Bronco)

4. *Mariposa Traicionera* (Maná)

5. *Como la Flor* (Selena)

6. *Sexo, Pudor, y Lágrimas* (Aleks Syntek)

7. *Triste Canción de Amor* (El Tri)

8. *Secreto de Amor* (Joan Sebastian)

9. *Tú Cárcel* (Los Bukis)

10. *Amor Eterno* (Juan Gabriel)

11. *Sabor a Mí* (Eydie Gorme y Los Panchos)

12. *Un Soñador* (Ada Chalino Sanchez)

13. *Inolvidable* (Luis Miguel)

14. *Entre Dos Tierras* (Heroes del Silencio)

15. Selections from *Pacto de Sangre* (Los Tigres del Norte)

16. *Contigo Sí* (Nadia and Yahir)

17. *Tal Vez* (Ricky Martin)

18. *Una Vez Más* (Conjunto Primavera)

19. *El Problema* (Ricardo Arjona)

20. *Amame* (Alexandre Pires)

21. *Así Es la Vida* (Olga Tañón)

22. *Que Me Quedes Tú* (Shakira)

23. *Sedúceme* (India)

24. Selections from *Sueños* (Intocable)

25. *En el 2000* (Natalia LaFourcade)

3 Ways to Pace Instruction with Beats per Minute (BPM)

Music revs up energy or calms people down, depending on its tempo. Choose music according to its beats per minute (BPM) to help you set the pace of an activity. Develop a sense for the effects of a song's tempo by listening to it first while relaxing in a chair and deciding if it speeds you up or slows you down.

1. *Slow.* Forty to sixty beats per minute calms an audience down. This music tempo is best for accompanying visualization, relaxation, journal writing, or reflection tasks.

2. *Moderate.* Sixty to seventy beats per minute maintains a steady alertness and sets a moderate pace for thinking or working on projects. It is also good background for solving problems and fostering creativity.

3. *Faster.* Seventy to one hundred forty beats per minute energizes a group. Fast music encourages movement, dance, and working on physical tasks (rather than mental ones). It spurs people productively towards a deadline.

7 Tips for Incorporating Rap into Learning

Turning instructional content into a rap song (the "opera of the streets") is easy to do. The melody or beat of a song carries the content, which makes it easier to remember. Provide a selection of song lyrics for the group to rewrite, or encourage more adventurous students to compose their own. (Be sure to screen the lyrics of the song first.) The following tips will help you easily incorporate rap into your presentation.

1. Allow students to work with partners.

2. Summarize the content by writing it out.

3. Identify key terms and concepts to use in the chorus or refrain.

4. Keep a rhyming dictionary on hand for reference.

5. Give "rap duos" time to practice and let them find quiet corners in which to perfect their performance.

6. Let learners choose between presenting their rap to the entire group or to a smaller group.

7. Require the listening audience to provide the performers with content feedback and stylistic feedback.

18 More Memorable Songs from the 1980s

I'm more than half a century old, so I've heard and danced to everything from the Swim, Twist, and Locomotion to line dancing and disco. But no decade in my memory cranked out as many catchy hits as the 1980s. Here are a few more goodies for your collection.

1. *Shake It Up* (The Cars)

2. *She's Sexy and 17* (The Stray Cats)

3. *Stepping Out* (Joe Jackson)

4. *One Thing Leads to Another* (The Fixx)

5. *Back on the Chain Gang* (The Pretenders)

6. *Vacation* (The Go-Gos)

7. *Our House* (Madness)

8. *Love Plus One* (Haircut 100)

9. *I Ran (So Far Away)* (A Flock of Seagulls)

10. *Everybody Wants to Rule the World* (Tears for Fears)

11. *Hold Me Now* (The Thompson Twins)

12. *You Can't Get What You Want* (Joe Jackson)

13. *My Ever Changing Moods* (Style Council)

14. *Break My Stride* (Matthew Wilder)

15. *Be Near Me* (ABC)

16. *Tenderness* (General Public)

17. *What I Like about You* (The Romantics)

18. *Don't Stop 'Til You Get Enough* (Michael Jackson)

10 Best Books on Music

You're already reading a book on music, so why would I suggest more? Because there are some that are pretty darn good. Some of the books on this list have a lot of research documentation, some are purely practical, and others are a mixture of both. I hope you find them useful.

1. *Handbook of Music Psychology, 2nd Edition* edited by Don Hodges (1996: IMR Press)

2. *The Ultimate Book of Music for Learning* by Rich Allen (Impact Learning)

3. *Music, the Brain, and Ecstasy: How Music Captures Our Imagination* by Robert Jourdain (1997: W. Morrow)

4. *Nurturing Your Child with Music* by John Ortiz (1999: Beyond Words Publishing)

5. *Keeping Mozart in Mind, 2nd Edition* by Gordon Shaw (2004: Elsevier)

6. *Top Tunes for Teaching* by Eric Jensen (2005: The Brain Store) (How could I resist?)

7. *The Mozart Effect* by Don Campbell (1997: Avon)

8. *The Green Book of Songs by Subject: The Thematic Guide to Popular Music, 5th Edition* by Jeff Green (2002: Professional Desk References)

9. *Good Music, Brighter Children* by Sharlene Habermeyer (1999: Prima Publishers)

10. *Music with the Brain in Mind* by Eric Jensen (2000: The Brain Store)

5 Music Selections that Prime the Brain for Learning

I think of priming as setting the brain up to learn. The ideal state for learning is probably relaxed alertness with a dash of curiosity and anticipation thrown in. Do you know any music selections that can do that? These five very diverse selections are a good starting point.

1. *Sonata in D Major for Two Pianos* (K448) (Mozart)

2. Compositions from *Music for Accelerated Learning* (Steven Halpern)

3. *Daphne et Chloe, Suite No. 2* (Ravel)

4. *Symphony in Three Movements* (Stravinsky)

5. Songs from *Laya Vinyas* (Indian drumming) (Trichy Sankaran)

6 Best Sound Systems for Playing Music

You should consider several factors before picking a music system to use during your presentations. In a first grade classroom, for example, issues like durability, economy, and safety might be important. A business trainer, however, might value more the quality of sound, ease of use, and a system's ability to fill a room. All of the units names below include a remote control, which is very important if you want to work from a distance. I personally like these six systems.

Best Quality for Less than $1,200

1. Bose Acoustic Wave CD player
2. Bose Acoustic Wave CD player with multi-disc changer

Excellent Quality for Less than $600

3. Bose Wave Radio/CD player

Good Quality for Less than $200

4. JVC RC-BM5 portable CD player
5. Panasonic RX-D23 portable CD player
6. Philips AZ1305 Boombox

7 Categories for Organizing Your Music

You'll never find all your tunes when you need them without some system of organization. May I suggest an idea? Organize them by purpose. Arrange your CD binder (or i-Pod selections) according to the categories below. You'll find music much faster when it is grouped by function rather than by artist. If, after you've been using music for a while, you find that these categories don't really fit the way you present, change them!

1. *Intermission* or *Break Music* (upbeat, familiar tunes with words)

2. *Background Selections* to accompany other activities (instrumental, predictable music from 60 to 70 BPM)

3. *Movement Jams* for physical games or mixers (exciting, high energy tunes of 120 BPM or faster)—see page 20 for ideas.

4. *Relaxation Selections* to calm a group down (instrumental music from 40 to 55 BPM)—see page 46 for ideas.

5. *Special Effects* for introductions, celebrations, funny moments, or group rituals (TV theme songs, game show sound effects, animal songs, and other novelty noises)—see page 52 for ideas.

6. *Start-Up Tunes* to call participants' attention back to the group or for great beginnings—see page 33 for ideas.

7. *Closing Selections* for sending everyone home or to the next class (songs with "good bye" in their lyrics)—see page 34 for ideas.

15 Tunes about Magic, Miracles, and Other Amazing Things

Play these positive, affirming selections for teamwork, projects, or problem-solving tasks. They send a clear message: We can all work miracles (when given the right support), so be a believer! These songs convey that message well. Just pick an artist and song that fits your particular instructional situation best.

1. *All I Need Is a Miracle* (Mike and the Mechanics)

2. *Miracle* (Bon Jovi)

3. *Higher* (Creed)

4. *Life Is So Good* (John Denver)

5. *Magic* (The Cars)

6. *Could It Be Magic* (Barry Manilow)

7. *With a Little Luck* (Paul McCartney)

8. *Every Little Thing She Does Is Magic* (The Police)

9. *When You Believe* (Mariah Carey and Whitney Houston)

10. *Do You Believe in Magic* (The Lovin' Spoonful)

11. *Impossible Dream* (Luther Vandross)

12. *It's a Miracle* (Barry Manilow)

13. *Miracles* (Jefferson Starship)

14. *You Can Do Magic* (America)

15. *Daydream Believer* (The Monkees)

13 Jammin' Hip-Hop Tunes

Although rap and hip-hop both began as urban cultural expressions, they have gone so mainstream that their audiences are global. (In fact, African-Americans buy less than twenty percent of all rap CDs.) So what's the appeal? Check out these current favorites, traditional rap tunes, and classics from this genre. (Remember to preview any songs you don't know before playing them for a group. Some artists don't fit every audience.)

1. *Crazy in Love* (Beyoncé)

2. *Hey Ya* (OutKast)

3. *Bootylicious* (Destiny's Child)

4. *Rapper's Delight* (The Sugarhill Gang)

5. *Miami* (Will Smith)

6. *U Can't Touch This* (MC Hammer)

7. *Funky Cold Medina* (Tone Loc)

8. *Bust a Move* (Young MC)

9. *Bananas* (Queen Latifah)

10. *Parents Just Don't Understand* (Lil' Romeo, 3LW, and Nick Cannon)

11. *Intergalactic Planetary* (The Beastie Boys)

12. *It Takes Two* (Fatman Scoop)

13. *You Talk Too Much* (Run-DMC)

10 Suggestions for Background Music

Music that is easy on the ears is best for the background. In fact, the more predictable a tune, the better. Splashy, unpredictable music makes its way into the foreground and diverts attention from the task at hand. When the brain knows what's coming musically, it can relax and work on other things while listening.

1. *Four Seasons* (Vivaldi)

2. Selections from *Whistle While You Work*
   (available from The Brain Store)

3. *Brandenburg Concertos* (J. S. Bach)

4. Environmental music featuring bird, ocean, flute, and waterfalls sounds

5. *Breezin'* (George Benson)

6. *Eine Kleine Nachtmusik* (Mozart)

7. Compositions from *Another World* (Harry Pickens)
   (available from The Brain Store)

8. Compositions from *Music for Accelerated Learning* (Steven Halpern)

9. Selections from *Natural States* (Lanz and Speer)

10. Selections from *More Whistle While You Work*
    (available from The Brain Store)

13 Tunes about Friendship and Teamwork

Use this music when you want to reinforce the power and importance of friendships. New songs or oldies, they strengthen the message that friends are important.

1. *We Are Family* (Sister Sledge)

2. *I'll Be There for You* (theme from *Friends*) (The Rembrandts)

3. *Endless Love* (Diana Ross and Lionel Ritchie)

4. *My Best Friend* (Tim McGraw)

5. *You've Got a Friend* (James Taylor)

6. *That's What Friends Are For* (Dionne Warwick)

7. *Love the One You're With* (Crosby, Stills, Nash, & Young)

8. *Shower the People* (James Taylor)

9. *Reach Out* (*I'll Be There*) (The Four Tops)

10. *Count On Me* (Whitney Houston)

11. *Let Your Love Flow* (The Bellamy Brothers)

12. *With a Little Help from My Friends* (The Beatles)

13. *Lean On Me* (Bill Withers)

18 Instrumentals for Brainstorming, Solving Problems, and Creativity

The selections on this list have spunk, variety, and flair. They also move quickly and have no words—perfect for keeping learners on their toes and thinking sharp.

1. *Piano Concerto No. 5 (Opus 73)* (Beethoven)

2. Any Etude by Chopin

3. Any Nocturne by Chopin

4. *Claire de Lune* (Debussy)

5. Compositions from *Another World* (Harry Pickens) (available from The Brain Store)

6. *Piano Concerto No. 26 in D* (K537) (Mozart)

7. *Piano Concerto No. 27 in B-Flat Major* (K595) (Mozart)

8. *Waltz* from *Swan Lake* (Tchaikovsky)

9. *Rhapsody in Blue* (Gershwin)

10. Selections from *In the Wake of the Wind* (David Arkenstone)

11. *Sonata for Two Pianos in D Major* (K448) (Mozart)

12. *Egmont Overture* (Opus 84) (Beethoven)

13. *Also Sprach Zarathustra* (The theme from *2001: A Space Odyssey*) (Richard Strauss)

14. *Blue Danube Waltz* (Johann Strauss)

15. Selections from *Fantasia* (Disney)

16. *Suites for Orchestra 1–4* (BWV1066–1069) (J. S. Bach)

17. *Toy Symphony* (Angerer*)

18. *A Musical Joke* (K522) (Mozart)

*This composition has been attributed variously to Franz Joseph Haydn, Michael Haydn, and Leopold Mozart, but recent research by Hildegard Herrmann-Schneider published in the journal, *Mozart Jahrbuch*, credits it to the Benedictine monk Father Edmund Angerer (1740–1794), who originally titled the composition, *Berchtoldsgaden Musick*.

16 Favorite 1970s Disco & Dance Tunes

Disco never dies. Sure, tunes from the 1970s could be corny, but they're still so popular that modern artists keep covering these favorite hits! This is another list that could have gone on forever.

1. *Stayin' Alive* (The Bee Gees)

2. *Love Rollercoaster* (The Ohio Players)

3. *I Will Survive* (Gloria Gaynor)

4. *(Shake, Shake, Shake) Shake Your Booty* (KC and the Sunshine Band)

5. *Last Dance* (Donna Summer)

6. *Dance, Dance, Dance* (Chic)

7. *Don't Leave Me This Way* (Thelma Houston)

8. *Macho Man* (The Village People)

9. *Ladies Night* (Kool and the Gang)

10. *December, 1963 (Oh, What a Night)* (The Four Seasons)

11. *I Love the Nightlife* (Alicia Bridges)

12. *Boogie Fever* (The Sylvers)

13. *Dancing Queen* (ABBA)

14. *Rock the Boat* (The Hues Corporation)

15. *Boogie Nights* (Heatwave)

16. *Disco Inferno* (The Trammps)

5 Ways to Use Music in the Classroom

1. *Introductions*. Music is a great way to introduce a person or upcoming event. It sets the tone and establishes a state of anticipation.

2. *Building Community*. Singing favorite songs together helps the whole group find common ground and create community. Singing also puts everyone into the same emotional state for an upcoming activity.

3. *Learn About*. Play music from an historical era to enhance knowledge about that time. Music relates information about history, romance, social events, politics, entertainment, and even science. Somewhere, someone has recorded a song about the topic you are presenting—you just have to look for it.

4. *Memory*. Experiment with music and memory in the classroom. Have students review assignments, like spelling lists, with instrumental music playing in the background. Then, repeat this activity another day without music and compare their performance on subsequent spelling tests.

5. *Presentation*. Use music to convey information and aid memory creation. Choose a familiar melody and write song lyrics to help students memorize a list of facts or some other assignment that requires verbal memory skills. Or, assign to students the task of writing their own songs for review.

19 Sweet, Loving, Romantic Songs

When you're in the mood, nothing's better. Playing these tunes will help you remember the first time you fell in love.

1. *Tonight* from *West Side Story* (Bernstein/Sondheim)

2. *Endless Love* (Diana Ross and Lionel Ritchie)

3. *Lady* (Kenny Rogers)

4. *Love Me Tender* (Elvis)

5. *Stand by Me* (Ben E. King)

6. *Fly Me to the Moon* (Bobby Darin)

7. *(You're My) Soul and Inspiration* (Righteous Brothers)

8. *My Guy* (Mary Wells)

9. *I Just Called to Say I Love You* (Stevie Wonder)

10. *Wonderful Tonight* (Eric Clapton)

11. *I've Got a Great Idea* (Harry Connick, Jr.)

12. *Moon River* (Andy Williams)

13. *The Night I Fell in Love* (Luther Vandross)

14. *As I Lay Me Down* (Sophie B. Hawkins)

15. *You and I* (Eddie Rabbit and Crystal Gayle)

16. *Loving You* (Minnie Riperton)

17. *At Last* (Etta James)

18. *You're in My Heart* (Rod Stewart)

19. *You Make Me Feel Brand New* (Roberta Flack)

15 Soothing, Inspiring Tunes

Listen to these compositions and albums while kicking back on a Sunday afternoon, relaxing after work, or planning your future. They lift, inspire, and, most of all, put you in a state of grace. Each composition has its own personality to meet any mood you are in.

1. *Aerial Boundaries* (Michael Hedges)

2. *Trois Gymnopédies* (Eric Satie)

3. *Peace and Quiet* (Harry Pickens) (available from The Brain Store)

4. *Solid Colors* (Liz Story)

5. *Morning* from *Peer Gynt Suite No. 1* (Greig)

6. *Goldberg Variations* (BWV988) (J. S. Bach)

7. *Spirit of Olympia* (David Arkenstone and Kostia)

8. *Music for Airports* (Brian Eno)

9. *Inner Rhythms* (Randy Crafton)

10. *Oh, What a Beautiful Morning* (Daniel Kobialka)

11. *Pianoscapes* (Michael Jones)

12. *Desert Vision* (Lanz and Speer)

13. *Instrumental Escape—Volume 5* (Medhi)

14. *Natural States* (Lanz and Speer)

15. *Air on the G String* (J. S. Bach)

14 Motown Favorites

Motown got its start in the 1960s in Detroit (the motor town) and the name became an anthem of sorts that celebrated the African-American urban landscape. It brought into popular culture the voices of many musicians who for too long had not been heard. Classy and dignified, these recording artists dressed and presented themselves like royalty.

1. *Respect* (Aretha Franklin)

2. *My Girl* (The Temptations)

3. *I Can't Help Myself (Sugarpie, Honeybunch)* (The Four Tops)

4. *Superstition* (Stevie Wonder)

5. *Heat Wave* (Martha and the Vandellas)

6. *The Tracks of My Tears* (Smokey Robinson)

7. *Walk On By* (Dionne Warwick)

8. *Midnight Train to Georgia* (Gladys Knight and the Pips)

9. *Brick House* (The Commodores)

10. *Baby Love* (Diana Ross and the Supremes)

11. *How Sweet It Is (To Be Loved by You)* (Marvin Gaye)

12. *Rescue Me* (Fontella Bass)

13. *Soul Man* (Sam & Dave)

14. *Higher and Higher* (Jackie Wilson)

22 Very Sure-Bet Albums for Smooth Jazz Listening

Many people have asked me about the genre of smooth jazz. It is intended, for the most part, to be comfortable, predictable, and mellow. These qualities make it great background music. However electric these jazz artists may be in concert, the albums on this list are perfect for supporting a quiet, studious environment.

1. *Best of George Benson* (George Benson)

2. *The Very Best of Acoustic Alchemy* (Acoustic Alchemy)

3. *Feels so Good* (Chuck Mangione)

4. *Collection* (Spyro Gyra)

5. *Urban Gypsy* (Marc Antoine)

6. *Tourist in Paradise* (The Rippingtons)

7. *Northern Nights* (Dan Siegel)

8. *Cruisin'* (Marc Antoine)

9. *Time Again* (David Sanborn)

10. *Silhouette* (Kenny G)

11. *Ricochet* (Richard Elliot)

12. *Mister Magic* (Grover Washington, Jr.)

13. *Night Creatures* (Tom Scott)

14. *One Quiet Night* (Pat Metheny)

15. *The Song Lives On* (Joe Sample and Lalah Hathaway)

16. *Take it From the Top* (Bob James)

17. *Mountain Dance* (Dave Grusin)

18. *Late Night Guitar* (Earl Klugh)

19. *Heartfelt* (Fourplay)

20. *Sapphire Blue* (Larry Carlton)

21. *Confidential* (Peter White)

22. *Esperanto* (Rick Braun)

19 Top R&B and Soul Oldies

Although not everyone will agree that these tunes are the best recordings of the best rhythm and blues artists, they are classics. You can't go wrong with any of these selections!

1. *Higher and Higher* (Jackie Wilson)

2. *Proud Mary* (Ike & Tina Turner)

3. *Tired of Being Alone* (Al Green)

4. *I Feel Good* (James Brown)

5. *(Sittin' On) The Dock of the Bay* (Otis Redding)

6. *I Heard It through the Grapevine* (Marvin Gaye)

7. *Can't Get Enough of Your Love, Babe* (Barry White)

8. *Woman's Gotta Have It* (Bobby Womack)

9. *Cupid* (Sam Cooke)

10. *Land of a Thousand Dances* (Wilson Pickett)

11. *Superfly* (Curtis Mayfield)

12. *Sweet Soul Music* (Arthur Conley)

13. Theme song from *Shaft* (Isaac Hayes)

14. *Maybelline* (Chuck Berry)

15. *Show and Tell* (Al Wilson)

16. *Spanish Harlem* (Ben E. King)

17. *Respect* (Aretha Franklin)

18. *Cry to Me* (Solomon Burke)

19. *Hit the Road, Jack* (Ray Charles)

12 Triumphant Tunes for Celebrating Successes

These selections will amplify feelings of success if you play them in the background during a celebration for significant classroom achievements. But don't overuse them—they will seem trite after a while.

1. *The Best* (Tina Turner)

2. *Hot! Hot! Hot!* (Buster Poindexter)

3. *I'm So Excited* (The Pointer Sisters)

4. *Ode to Joy* from the *Ninth Symphony* (Beethoven)

5. *Celebrate* (Three Dog Night)

6. *Grand March* from *Aida* (Verdi)

7. *Celebration* (Kool and the Gang)

8. *Holiday* (Madonna)

9. *Gonna Fly Now* (The theme from *Rocky*)
   (Bill Conti and Maynard Ferguson)

10. *We Are the Champions* (Queen)

11. *Zip-A-Dee-Doo-Dah* from Disney's *Song of the South*
    (Wrubel/Gilbert)

12. *Hallelujah Chorus* from *Messiah* (Handel)

16 Playful Songs about School

Match the lyrics of these songs to the goals you have in mind for your presentation—you always want to send students the right message about learning, school, and teachers!

1. *School's Out* (Alice Cooper)

2. *Teach Your Children Well* (Crosby, Stills, Nash, & Young)

3. *School Days* (Chuck Berry)

4. *Teach the Gifted Children* (Lou Reed)

5. *The Teacher* (Paul Simon)

6. *School Is In* (Gary US Bonds)

7. *Me and Julio Down by the School Yard* (Paul Simon)

8. *Be True to Your School* (The Beach Boys)

9. *Don't Know Much about History* (Herman's Hermits)

10. *To Sir with Love* (Lulu)

11. *Rock 'n' Roll High School* (The Ramones)

12. *School* (SuperTramp)

13. *No More Homework* (Gary U. S. Bonds)

14. *High School Confidential* (Jerry Lee Lewis)

15. *High School Dance* (The Sylvers)

16. *Harper Valley PTA* (Loretta Lynn)

1️⃣0️⃣ Rockin' Ways to Introduce Something Cool

These pieces all make great set-up music. Use them first to create a strong anticipatory state. Then, immediately follow them up with something positive (to keep the mood and maintain your credibility).

1. Theme song from *The Flintstones* (Curtin/Hanna & Barbera)

2. *New Attitude* (Patti LaBelle)

3. *Fanfare for the Common Man* (Aaron Copland)

4. *Tell Me Something Good* (Rufus)

5. *Gonna Fly Now* (the theme from *Rocky*) (Bill Conti and Maynard Ferguson)

6. Theme from the 1984 Summer Olympics (John Williams)

7. Theme from *Star Wars* (John Williams)

8. *We Will Rock You* (Queen)

9. *Triumphal March* from *Aida* (Verdi)

10. Theme from *Indiana Jones* (John Williams)

21 Perfect Conclusion Tunes

Whether you're at the end of a single forty-five-minute class, a full-day class, or a week-long conference, closing songs are important. They help solidify the mood and send everyone home with a good feeling. As expected, use different tunes for different occasions, cultures, and moods.

1. *Heigh-Ho* from Disney's *Snow White* (Frank Churchill)

2. *What a Wonderful World* (Louis Armstrong)

3. *I've Had the Time of My Life* (Bill Medley and Jennifer Warnes)

4. *Five O'Clock World* (The Vogues)

5. *Is It Over Yet* (Wynonna)

6. *Happy Trails* (Dale Evans)

7. *Good Riddance (Time of Your Life)* (Green Day)

8. *See You Later, Alligator* (Bill Haley and His Comets)

9. *Leaving on a Jet Plane* (Peter, Paul, & Mary)

10. *So Long, Farewell* from *The Sound of Music* (Rodgers/Hammerstein)

11. *Adios, Amigo* (Jim Reeves)

12. *Tomorrow* from *Annie* (Strouse/Charnin)

13. *Hit the Road, Jack* (Ray Charles)

14. *Bye, Bye, Bye* ('N Sync)

15. *Na Na Hey Hey Kiss Him Goodbye* (Steam)

16. *If You Leave* (OMD)

17. *If You Leave* (Destiny's Child)

18. *Baby Don't Go* (Sonny & Cher)

19. *Closing Time* (SemiSonic)

20. *Auld Lang Syne* (Patti LaBelle)

21. *Who Let the Dogs Out* (The Baha Men)

21 More 1980s Dance Hits

All of the songs on this list have a catchy beat, good lyrics, and are totally fun songs for countless uses.

1. *Our Lips Are Sealed* (The Go-Gos)

2. *Mexican Radio* (Wall of Voodoo)

3. *Only a Lad* (Oingo Boingo)

4. *The Future's So Bright I Gotta Wear Shades* (Timbuk 3)

5. *Save It for Later* (English Beat)

6. *Mad about You* (Belinda Carlisle)

7. *Tenderness* (General Public)

8. *Rain in the Summertime* (The Alarm)

9. *Our House* (Madness)

10. *Dance Hall Days* (Wang Chung)

11. *Rock This Town* (The Stray Cats)

12. *Jessie's Girl* (Rick Springfield)

13. *The Walls Came Down* (The Call)

14. *Call Me* (Blondie)

15. *What I Like about You* (The Romantics)

16. *Electric Avenue* (Eddy Grant)

17. *Politics of Dancing* (Re-Flex)

18. *We Got the Beat* (The Go-Gos)

19. *Tainted Love* (Soft Cell)

20. *The Safety Dance* (Men Without Hats)

21. *I Melt with You* (Modern English)

18 Pumped-Up, High-Energy Jams

These artists dare you to stand still! This music is so on fire that you can't listen to it while sitting.

1. *I Like to Move It* (Reel 2 Reel)

2. *Tiki Dance* (Fenua)

3. *Neutron Dance* (The Pointer Sisters)

4. *Let's Get Ready to Rumble* (Michael Buffer)

5. *Goody Two Shoes* (Adam Ant)

6. *La Bamba* (Ritchie Valens)

7. *U Can't Touch This* (MC Hammer)

8. *Hot, Hot, Hot* (Arrow)

9. *C'Mon 'n Ride It (The Train)* (The Quad City DJs)

10. *I'm So Excited* (The Pointer Sisters)

11. *Whip It* (Devo)

12. *Shake It Up* (The Cars)

13. *Great Balls of Fire* (Jerry Lee Lewis)

14. *Another Night* (Real McCoy)

15. *You Ain't Seen Nothing Yet* (BTO)

16. *Can Can* (Bad Manners)

17. *Jump* (Van Halen)

18. *Eye of the Tiger* (Survivor)

22 Highly Affirming, Super-Positive, Optimistic Tunes

These are classics for putting a group into a good mood or cheering yourself up.

1. *The Impossible Dream* from *Man of La Mancha* (Leigh/Darion)

2. *Let the Good Times Roll* (Ray Charles)

3. *One Fine Day* (The Chiffons)

4. *Hold Your Head Up* (Argent)

5. *Shout* (The Isley Brothers)

6. *Ac-cent-tchu-ate the Positive* (Bing Crosby)

7. *I Feel Good* (James Brown)

8. *Singing in the Rain* from *Singing the Rain* (Brown/Freed)

9. *Shining Star* (Earth, Wind, & Fire)

10. *Be Happy* (Mary J. Blige)

11. *Good Times Roll* (The Cars)

12. *It's So Easy* (Buddy Holly)

13. *Life's Been Good* (The Eagles)

14. *This Kiss* (Faith Hill)

15. *Good Times* (Chic)

16. *Anything Goes* from *Anything Goes* (Cole Porter)

17. *You Can Make It If You Try* (Sly and the Family Stone)

18. *Hawaiian Roller Coaster Ride* from Disney's *Lilo & Stitch* (Silvestri/Bifano)

19. *Happy Together* (The Turtles)

20. *Still the One* (Orleans)

21. *If You're Happy and You Know It* (Traditional)

22. *For Once in My Life* (Stevie Wonder)

13 Contemporary R&B Artists

Here is a list of contemporary R&B (rhythm and blues) favorites.

1. *Break Up 2 Make Up* (Ashanti)

2. *I Care 4 U* (Aaliyah)

3. *Booti Call* (Blackstreet)

4. *On Bended Knee* (Boyz II Men)

5. *The Boy Is Mine* (Brandy)

6. *Lady Marmalade* (Christina Aguilera)

7. *Jumpin' Jumpin'* (Destiny's Child)

8. *Dreams* (Gabrielle)

9. *No Time Like the Future* (Incognito)

10. *Dance with my Father* (Luther Vandross)

11. *Heartbreaker* (Mariah Carey)

12. *Family Affair* (Mary J. Blige)

13. *Waterfalls* (TLC)

23 Smokin' Hot Dance Hits of the 1990s

You've got to agree that the songs of the 1980s and 1990s are some of the most fun dance tunes ever recorded. You can understand the words, the beat is strong—they're irresistible.

1. *Ooh Aah (Just a Little Bit)* (Gina G)

2. *Ray of Light* (Madonna)

3. *All Star* (Smash Mouth)

4. *Another Night* (Real McCoy)

5. *The Sign* (Ace of Base)

6. *Just a Girl* (No Doubt)

7. *Unbelievable* (EMF)

8. *Touch Me* (Cathy Dennis)

9. *Jellyhead* (Crush)

10. *Electric Barbarella* (Duran Duran)

11. *Runaround* (Blues Traveler)

12. *Boom Shak-a-Lak* (Apache Indian)

13. *Feels Like I'm in Love* (Kelly Marie)

14. *Boom, Boom, Boom* (Outhere Brothers)

15. *What Is Love* (Haddaway)

16. *Everybody Everybody* (Black Box)

17. *Be My Lover* (La Bouche)

18. *The Cup of Life* (Ricky Martin)

19. *U Can't Touch This* (MC Hammer)

20. *Un-Break My Heart* (Toni Braxton)

21. *Step by Step* (Whitney Houston)

22. *Kiss You All Over* (No Mercy)

23. *Whoomp (There It Is)* (Tag Team)

20 Workshop Interactives: Find-a-Partner Songs

I use music as part of a stand up or paired sharing activity. These songs make getting into this kind of activity a little more fun. Play music when you introduce each segment of the task.

Finding a Partner

1. *Get On Up* (The Esquires)

2. *Get Up, Stand Up* (Bob Marley)

3. *I'm Walking* (Fats Domino)

4. *Ain't Too Proud to Beg* (The Temptations)

5. *Do Ya Think I'm Sexy* (Rod Stewart)

6. *Shop Around* (Smokey Robinson and the Miracles)

7. *It Takes Two* (Marvin Gaye and Kim Weston)

Introducing Yourself

8. *Hello Dolly* (Louis Armstrong)

9. *Getting to Know You* from *The King & I* (Rodgers & Hammerstein)

10. *I Can't Get Next to You* (The Temptations)

11. Theme from *Mr. Ed* television show (Jay Livingston)

12. *Talk to Me* (Anita Baker)

13. *Big Shot* (Billy Joel)

14. *Hello* (Lionel Ritchie)

15. *Come a Little Bit Closer* (Fleetwood Mac)

16. *You've Got a Friend* (James Taylor)

17. *Hey, Good Lookin'* (Hank Williams)

18. *Why Can't We Be Friends* (War)

19. *Together Again* (Janet Jackson)

20. *Hello, I Love You* (The Doors)

20 More Workshop Interactives: With-Your-Partner Songs

I use music as part of a stand up or paired sharing activity. These songs make getting into this kind of activity a little more fun. Play music when you introduce each segment of the task.

Talking to Your Partner

1. *Tell Me Something Good* (Rufus)

2. *ABC* (Jackson 5)

3. *Sweet Talkin' Guy* (The Chiffons)

4. *Tell It Like It Is* (Aaron Neville)

5. *Everybody's Talkin'* (Harry Nilsson)

6. *You Talk Too Much* (Run-DMC)

7. *Don't Let Me Be Misunderstood* (The Animals)

8. *Yakety Yak* (The Coasters)

9. *You Got What It Takes* (Marv Johnson)

10. *A Little Less Talk and a Lot More Action* (Toby Keith)

11. *Don't Go Breaking My Heart* (Elton John and Kiki Dee)

Returning to Your Seat

12. *Get Back* (The Beatles)

13. *Hit the Road, Jack* (Ray Charles)

14. *Easy Come, Easy Go* (Elvis Presley)

15. *That's the Way (I Like It)* (KC and the Sunshine Band)

16. *Homeward Bound* (Simon & Garfunkel)

17. *Reunited* (Peaches & Herb)

18. *Breaking Up Is Hard to Do* (Neil Sedaka)

19. *Right Back Where We Started From* (Maxine Nightingale)

20. *Never Can Say Goodbye* (The Jackson 5)

22 Fun-Lovin' Extravaganzas

You have to admit that some songs are just flat-out sing-alongs. These tunes have playful content and very, very catchy "hooks" to them.

1. *Dancing in Street*
   (Martha and the Vandellas)

2. *Great Balls of Fire*
   (Jerry Lee Lewis)

3. *Rock Around the Clock*
   (Bill Haley and His Comets)

4. *Splish Splash* (Bobby Darin)

5. *I Can't Help Myself
   (Sugarpie, Honeybunch)*
   (The Four Tops)

6. *Yakety Yak* (The Coasters)

7. *Hooked on a Feeling* (Blue Suede)

8. *Palisades Park* (Freddy Cannon)

9. *Pretty Woman* (Roy Orbison)

10. *Locomotion* (Little Eva)

11. *That'd Be Alright* (Alan Jackson)

12. *Walking on Sunshine*
    (Katrina and the Waves)

13. *Soak Up the Sun* (Sheryl Crow)

14. *This Is It* (Kenny Loggins)

15. *Money in My Pocket*
    (Dennis Brown)

16. *Everybody Have Fun Tonight*
    (Wang Chung)

17. *Good Vibrations* (The Beach Boys)

18. *Shake Your Love* (Debbie Gibson)

19. *I'm So Excited*
    (The Pointer Sisters)

20. *Still the One* (Orleans)

21. *Mad About You* (Belinda Carlisle)

22. *Summer Breeze* (Seals & Croft)

10 More Upbeat Energizers

If the teacher or trainer is excited, the enthusiasm rubs off on students. Wake up your brain, energize your body, and get your learners going with the following selections.

1. *Get On Up* (The Esquires)

2. *Walk Right In* (The Rooftop Singers)

3. *Jump* (Van Halen)

4. *Great Balls of Fire* (Jerry Lee Lewis)

5. *Do Wah Diddy Diddy* (Manfred Mann)

6. *Blue Suede Shoes* (Carl Perkins) (or the version by Elvis)

7. *Rock 'n' Roll Music* (Chuck Berry) (or the version by the Beatles)

8. *At the Hop* (Danny and the Juniors)

9. *Locomotion* (Little Eva) (or the version by Kylie Minogue)

10. Selections from *Hooked on Classics* (Philadelphia Harmonics)

7 Top "Girl Power" Songs of All Time

It's good to play songs that pump you up every now and then. I hope you have fun with these songs.

1. *I Am Woman* (Helen Reddy)

2. *Respect* (Aretha Franklin)

3. *I Will Survive* (Gloria Gaynor)

4. *(I've Got) The Power* (Snap)

5. *You Make Me Feel Like a Natural Woman* (Aretha Franklin)

6. *Wild Women Do* (Natalie Cole)

7. *Girls Just Wanna Have Fun* (Cyndi Lauper)

47 Popular Artists with "Explicit Lyrics" Albums

Once you start using music in your presentations, learners will probably approach you with songs or CDs they'd like you to play. Many of the songs you hear on the radio are "clean" versions of songs that appear on albums—some with very explicit, adult, or violent lyrics that you would not want to play in front of a group. You may recognize many of the artists on this from their hits on mainstream radio but realize that not every song they sing can be rated "G."

1. 2Pac
2. 50 Cent
3. 311
4. Beastie Boys
5. Blink 182
6. Bone Thugs-n-Harmony
7. Cypress Hill
8. De La Soul
9. DMX
10. Dr. Dre
11. Eazy Duz It
12. Eminem
13. Everlast
14. Funkmaster Flex
15. Guns N' Roses
16. Ice Cube
17. Janet Jackson
18. Jay Z
19. Kid Rock
20. Korn
21. LL Cool J
22. Lil' Kim
23. Limp Bizkit
24. Liz Phair
25. Ludacris
26. Madonna
27. Metallica
28. Missy Elliott
29. Mobb Deep
30. Nas
31. Naughty by Nature
32. Nelly
33. Nine Inch Nails
34. NWA and the Posse
35. Offspring
36. OutKast
37. R. Kelly
38. Rage Against the Machine
39. Rancid
40. Red Hot Chili Peppers
41. Run-DMC
42. Smashing Pumpkins
43. Snoop Doggy Dog
44. Sublime
45. Tool
46. Wu Tang Clan
47. Xzibit

23 More Positive, Inspirational Songs

Face it. We can all use some more positive messages in our life. These classic tunes will cheer up your group as well as brighten your own day.

1. *Don't Worry, Be Happy* (Bobby McFerrin)

2. *Yes, We Can Can* (The Pointer Sisters)

3. *Good Morning, Good Morning* (The Beatles)

4. *All I Wanna Do* (Sheryl Crow)

5. *I'm into Something Good* (Herman's Hermits)

6. Theme from *Happy Days* (Pratt/McClain)

7. *Oh! What a Beautiful Morning* from *Oklahoma* (Rodgers/Hammerstein)

8. *Fun, Fun, Fun* (The Beach Boys)

9. *You Are the Sunshine of My Life* (Stevie Wonder)

10. *Everything Is Beautiful* (Ray Stevens)

11. *One Fine Day* (The Chiffons)

12. *Have a Good Time* (Paul Simon)

13. *Over the Rainbow* (IZ)

14. *Wonderful! Wonderful!* (Johnny Mathis)

15. *Hot Fun in the Summertime* (Sly and the Family Stone)

16. *New Attitude* (Patti LaBelle)

17. *Good Feeling to Know* (Poco)

18. *Put on a Happy Face* from *Bye Bye Birdie* (Strouse/Adams)

19. *I'll Take You There* (The Staple Singers)

20. *Take It Easy* (The Eagles)

21. *Born Free* (Matt Monroe)

22. *Higher & Higher* (Jackie Wilson)

23. *Tomorrow* from *Annie* (Strouse/Charnin)

17 Albums to Calm the Mind and Soothe the Body

A quiet moment for stretching and deep breathing relieves physical and mental stress—ask a volunteer to lead your group through a few postures. Selections from these albums make wonderful accompaniment for your routine. These pieces also help clear the mind for the new learning that follows.

1. Any of the "Seasons" albums by George Winston

2. *Mandala* (Kitaro)

3. *Mosaic: The Best of John Klemmer* (John Klemmer)

4. *Serenity Suite: Music and Nature* (Steven Halpern)

5. *Devotion: The Best of Yanni* (Yanni)

6. *Cristofori's Dream* (David Lanz)

7. *Chrysalis* (2002)

8. *Oh, What a Beautiful Morning* (Daniel Kobialka)

9. *Paint the Sky with Stars* (Enya)

10. *CinemOcean* (Anastasi)

11. *Somewhere in a Dream* (Hisham)

12. *Seapeace* (Georgia Kelly)

13. *Peace and Quiet* (Harry Pickens)

14. *Chopin: The Complete Nocturnes* (performed by Claudio Arrau)

15. *Deep Breakfast* (Ray Lynch)

16. *Common Ground* (Paul Winter)

17. *The Magic of Satie* (performed by Jean-Yves Thibaudet)

16 More Exceedingly Upbeat and Happy Tunes

These tunes are both upbeat and have a great rhythm. Need more positive music in your life? Here it is!

1. *Walking on Sunshine* (Katrina and the Waves)

2. *Easy* (The Commodores)

3. *Everybody Is a Star* (Sly and the Family Stone)

4. *Good Vibrations* (The Beach Boys)

5. *Happy Jack* (The Who)

6. *I Like It* (Gerry and the Pacemakers)

7. *Everything's Coming Up Roses* from *Gypsy* (Styne/Sondheim)

8. *The In Crowd* (Dobie Gray)

9. *Beautiful Morning* (The Rascals)

10. *Glad All Over* (Dave Clark Five)

11. *That's the Way (I Like It)* (KC and the Sunshine Band)

12. *When You're Smiling* (Louis Armstrong) (or the version by Frank Sinatra)

13. *I Feel Fine* (The Beatles)

14. *What One Man Can Do* (John Denver)

15. *Getting Better* (The Beatles)

16. *59th Street Bridge Song (Feelin' Groovy)* (Simon & Garfunkel)

11 "Warp-Speed" Tunes for Beating a Deadline

Instead of hounding and cajoling my audience to hurry up, I simply announce, "You have three minutes"—or however much time remains—"to finish this task." Then, I play one of these tunes. Believe me, things will get done fast.

1. *1812 Overture* (Tchaikovsky)

2. Theme from *Hawaii 5-0* (Morton Stevens)

3. Theme from *Miami Vice* (Jan Hammer)

4. *William Tell Overture* (Rossini)

5. Selections from *Transitions to Go* (available from The Brain Store)

6. *Chariots of Fire* (Vangelis)

7. *Pipeline* (The Chantays)

8. *Red River Rock* (Johnny and the Hurricanes)

9. *Walk—Don't Run* (The Ventures)

10. Selections from *Wake Up the Brain* (available from The Brain Store)

11. Theme from *The Bugs Bunny/Road Runner Hour* (Jay Livingston)

11 "Counting" Songs

These songs are good for youngsters learning to count, but they'll liven up any class and create a sense of anticipation.

1. *Rock Around the Clock* (Bill Haley and His Comets)

2. *Ten Little Indians*

3. *Ladybug's Picnic* from *Sesame Street*

4. *Twelve Days of Gym Class*
   (on the CD, *Physical Ed*, from The Learning Station)

5. *One-Potato-Two*

6. *Hickory Dickory Dock*

7. *Five Little Monkeys Jumping on the Bed*

8. *ABC* (Jackson Five)

9. *1-2-3* (Gloria Estefan and the Miami Sound Machine)

10. *Twelve Days of Christmas*

11. *Book of Love* (The Monotones)

21 Songs that Name a Day of the Week

Playing a song about a day of the week is not just clever—it makes your presentation more fun. The songs on this list can be played at the start of the day (or, on Fridays, at the end of it).

1. *Come Monday* (Jimmy Buffet)

2. *Monday, Monday* (The Mamas and the Papas)

3. *Blue Monday* (Fats Domino) (or the version by Bobby Darin)

4. *Rainy Days and Mondays* (The Carpenters)

5. *Manic Monday* (The Bangles)

6. *Ruby Tuesday* (The Rolling Stones)

7. *Tuesday Afternoon* (The Moody Blues)

8. *Tuesday's Dead* (Cat Stevens)

9. *Wednesday Morning, 3 AM* (Simon & Garfunkel)

10. *Thursday* (Jim Croce)

11. *Friday on My Mind* (David Bowie)

12. *Friday I'm in Love* (The Cure)

13. *Another Saturday Night* (Sam Cooke)

14. *Saturday in the Park* (Chicago)

15. *Saturday Night* (The Eagles)

16. *Saturday Night's Alright (For Fighting)* (Elton John)

17. *Sunday Morning Coming Down* (Johnny Cash)

18. *Never on Sunday* (Andy Williams)

19. *Pleasant Valley Sunday* (The Monkees)

20. *Sunday Papers* (Joe Jackson)

21. *Workin' for the Weekend* (Ken Mellons)

17 Instrumental Pieces that Sizzle

I use instrumentals for background when people are talking during an activity. They work great for a ball toss game, cleaning up, or moving things around. Because instrumentals have no words, they have a positive effect. Every song on this list is a sure-fire tune that will get your audience—young or old—up and moving.

1. *Guitar Boogie Shuffle* (The Virtues)

2. *Teen Beat* (Sandy Nelson)

3. *Memphis* (Lonnie Mack)

4. *Red River Rock* (Johnny and the Hurricanes)

5. *Java* (Al Hirt)

6. *Tequila* (The Champs)

7. *Grazing in the Grass* (Hugh Masekela)

8. *Soulful Strut* (Young Holt Limited)

9. *A Swinging Safari* (Billy Vaughn and His Orchestra)

10. *Watermelon Man* (Mongo Santamaria)

11. *Linus and Lucy* (The theme from *Peanuts*) (Vince Guaraldi)

12. *William Tell Overture* (Rossini)

13. *Oh Yeah!* (Yello)

14. *Ride of the Valkyries* (Wagner)

15. *Gypsy Baron March* (Johann Strauss, Jr.)

16. *Wedding March Mazurka* (Opus 20a) (Tchaikovsky)

17. *In the Mood* (Glen Miller)

5 Best Specialty CDs to Buy

In an era of instant downloads, are there any whole CDs worth buying? Yes! You don't always want to acquire songs one or two at a time—sometimes you need the whole CD. The following list of items (naturally, I find The Brain Store CDs useful) is of albums good enough to use in every presentation that you give.

1. *Jazzy Tunes for Trainers* (Trainer's Warehouse)

2. *Television's Greatest Hits* (multi-volume series) (TvT)

3. *Wake Up the Brain* (The Brain Store)

4. *Wake Up the Young Brain* (The Brain Store)

5. *Transitions to Go!* (The Brain Store)

7 Highly Essential Special Effects

Special effects are harder to find than your run-of-the-mill song. An Internet search will bring up a lot of them for you; you can find more on special CD compilations. I use at least two of the following effects in every presentation I make.

1. Theme from *Dragnet* (Walter Schumann)

2. Theme from *Jeopardy* (Merv Griffin)

3. Theme song from *The Flintstones* (Curtin/Hanna & Barbera)

4. Theme from *The Twilight Zone* (Bernard Hermann)

5. Theme from *Mission Impossible* (Lalo Schifrin)

6. *The Stripper* (David Rose and His Orchestra)

7. Theme from *The Pink Panther* (Henry Mancini)

9 Solutions to Listeners' Complaints about <u>Your</u> Music

Before you play music:

1. Realize ahead of time that you can't please everybody.

2. Set ground rules about music ahead of time—discuss who has permission to handle the music system, CDs, or other tools you use.

3. Be consistent with your rules and treatment of others.

4. Acknowledge and respect the various needs of your learners. Thank them politely for their input.

If someone complains:

5. Is the volume too high? Listeners are likely to complain about any music if they can't hear what you are saying.

6. Reassure auditory learners that playing the music is for temporary effect. Consider letting them sit further from the speakers.

7. Always make your reasons for using music clear—why you use it, how you choose what to play, and how music assists learning.

8. Have ear plugs on hand to give out—they're cheap (and funny).

9. Avoid habituation. Vary the genre of music you play and use music for less than half of your instruction time.

Periods of Western Music

Not all old music is classical. Here's a timeline for quick reference about the music that predates Madonna and Sting.

1. *Medieval (before 1500 AD)*
   Gregorian chants, flutes, and bells

2. *Renaissance (1500–1600)*
   Lots of tambourines, percussion, drums, bells, and chimes

3. *Baroque (1600–1750)*
   Horns, organs, harpsichords, and wind instruments

4. *Classical (1750–1820)*
   Appearance of the piano and the modern-day full orchestra

5. *Early Romantic (1820–1860)*
   Suspenseful, emotional, and joyful

6. *Late Romantic (1860–1900)*
   Lots of strings, oboe, and percussion

7. *1900–1950*
   Chamber music, marches, ragtime, Dixieland, gospel, jazz, and big band

8. *1950–present*
   Everything!

5 Baroque Composers (1600-1750)

Music of this era was simple, ornamental, and regal. The dominant instruments were horns and strings, with some keyboard instruments. This music is best used in the background, to promote harmony and restful alertness. It is characterized by balance, unity, and counterpoint. Most composers were permanently employed by a church, court, council, or opera house. They wrote music for specific occasions and the music usually glorified God, the king, or a particular event. The following five Baroque composers are listed with one of their most famous compositions.

1. Antonio Vivaldi—*Four Seasons*

2. Johann Sebastian Bach—*Brandenburg Concertos*

3. George Frideric Handel—*Water Music*

4. Georg Philipp Telemann—*Le Triomphe de l'Amour*

5. Arcangelo Corelli—*Concerti Grossi*

5 Classical Composers (1750-1820)

Classical music could be characterized as the first "rock" music in history; it is full of energy, surprise, and contrast. Classical music hatched the modern orchestra, the symphony, themes and motives, the sonata, the concerto, and the overture. Play it to support creativity, in the background, or during storytelling and lectures. Classical composers were usually supported by a patron who provided financial backing in exchange for publicity, ego gratification, and primary access to the compositions. The following five Classical composers are listed with one of their most famous compositions.

1. Wolfgang Amadeus Mozart—*Eine Kleine Nachtmusik*

2. Franz Joseph Hayden—*Symphony No. 48 in C*

3. Giaochino Rossini—*William Tell Overture*

4. Ludwig van Beethoven—*Fifth Symphony* (Opus 67 in C Minor)

5. Felix Mendelssohn—*Violin Concerto in E Minor* (Opus 64)

Romantic Composers (1820-1900)

Music of this era is characterized by passion, suspense, wonder, impulse, ecstasy, and depth. Expect it to trigger a sense of freedom with connotations of the fictitious, far off, legendary, fantastic, or surreal. You've heard a great deal of Romantic music as the background for movie themes and Disney animations. The music can set the stage for emotions, clear out anger, and arouse interest and curiosity. It can announce an arrival, help us to fall in love, evoke rage, signal depression, or underscore a chase scene. The following nine Romantic composers are listed with one of their most famous compositions.

1. Franz Schubert—*Marche Militaire No. 1*

2. Pytor Ilyich Tchaikovsky—*1812 Overture*

3. Frederick Chopin—any mazurka or polonaise (two musical genre he invented)

4. Richard Wagner—*Ride of the Valkyries*

5. Giuseppe Verdi—*La Traviata*

6. Antonin Dvorak—*Symphony No. 9 in E Minor (From the New World)*

7. Nicolai Rimsky-Korsakov—*Flight of the Bumblebee*

8. Claude Debussy—*Suite "Bergamasque"*

9. Johannes Brahms—*German Requiem*

7 Contemporary Composers (1900-present)

"Contemporary" music includes not only the popular composers who write for night clubs, the radio, and movies, but also the more "artistic" composers who are frequently lumped with their Baroque, Classical, and Romantic predecessors. Contemporary music is a much freer structure, containing elements from irregular rhythms and new harmonies to the experimentation with ordinary objects to produce musical sounds. The following seven Contemporary composers are listed with one of their most famous compositions.

1. Igor Stravinsky—*Sacre du Printemps (The Rite of Spring)*

2. Dmitri Shostakovich—*Preludes and Fugues for Piano* (Opus 87)

3. Gustav Mahler—*Eighth Symphony*

4. Gustav Holst—*The Planets*

5. Bela Bartok—*Hungarian Folk Songs*

6. John Cage—*Imaginary Landscapes*

7. Arnold Schoenberg—*Verklarte Nacht* (Opus 4)

 Favorite Early American Composers

Early American composers stood on the shoulders of the giants of the past to create entirely new music forms. The great marches, ragtime, and sweeping waltzes all come out of this explosive musical era. Such music evokes grandeur, emotion, humor, and excitement. The following six composers are listed with one of their most famous compositions.

1. John Phillips Sousa—*Stars and Stripes Forever*

2. George Gershwin—*Rhapsody in Blue*

3. Scott Joplin—*Maple Leaf Rag*

4. Aaron Copland—*Rodeo*

5. Virgil Thomson—*5 Songs from William Blake*

6. Leonard Bernstein—*West Side Story*

Famous Big Band Tunes

Big band music was written as dance music for live audience performances, especially swing dancing. It's fun, upbeat, and happy—truly an oldie but goodie. It can be used with groups as break or recess music, or for background accompaniment during team projects.

1. *In the Mood* (Glen Miller)

2. *Take the "A" Train* (Duke Ellington)

3. *Sing, Sing, Sing* (Benny Goodman)

4. *Opus One* (Tommy Dorsey)

5. *I've Got My Love to Keep Me Warm* (Les Brown)

6. *Eager Beaver* (Stan Kenton)

7. *Stardust* (Artie Shaw)

22 Modern American Music Genres (1955–present)

It seems like the last fifty years have brought out more music forms than the last five hundred—an explosion of creativity. This list is to encourage you to listen to music outside your usual preferences. There are tons of great artists out there!

1. Nashville Sound

2. Traditional Jazz

3. Rock 'n' Roll

4. Christian Folk

5 Philadelphia Beat

6. California Sound

7. Country-Western

8. Modern Jazz

9. Motown

10. English Beat

11. New Wave

12. Jazz Fusion

13. Pop

14. Reggae

15. Soft Rock

16. Latina

17. Gospel

18. Smooth Jazz

19. Christian Rock

20. Rap

21. Country Rock

22. Hip-Hop

4 Ways Music Can Influence Cognition

Positive Influences

1. *Well-selected background music boosts creativity and arousal.* Background music can actually boost cognition during certain tasks. In creative situations, background music may increase bilateral cerebral arousal levels, possibly through the mediating role of the right hemisphere—the brain's center for creative and intuitive thinking (Morton et al., 1990). Background instrumental music played during low-level cognitive tasks improves verbal recall significantly more than vocal music (Nittono, 1997). Background music played during verbal discussions decreases anxiety, especially if the music is played in major keys (Blood & Ferris, 1993). The ideal background music is repetitive, familiar, instrumental, and played at a low to moderate volume.

2. *Rhythm helps with spatial tasks.* The original Mozart study showed—for the first time ever—a causal relationship between listening to music and cognition (see page 6 for more information about the findings from this study). If you have a task that requires spatial abstract reasoning (like object rotation, solving a visual spatial problem, designing something, or performing geometry), play rhythmic music first. It may help prime the brain for better performance. Study results have been mixed but generally affirming.

Negative Influences

3. *Competing vocals hurt cognition.* One study measured the speed at which college students wrote essays on a computer while exposed to low-level music. Participants were asked to complete a ten-minute writing task—half of them in silence and half of them with music; the music was either strictly instrumental or instrumental with vocals added. The researchers found that playing either type of musical compositions in the background reduced the subjects' writing speed by an average of ten words in ten minutes (6 percent)

as compared to control group. Writing quality, however, was not significantly affected. These findings may indicate that students listening to music while writing reduce their writing speed to maintain performance level.

4. *Stressful music impairs thinking time.* Music can be stressful in many ways. First, if the beat is too fast for an activity, it may create stress. Second, if a student dislikes the music, it may be stressful. Finally, if the music is too loud, too quiet, or of poor quality, it can be stressful. In short, think through what you're playing and why before you do it.

Blood, D. J. & Ferriss, S. J. (1993, Feb). Effects of background music on anxiety, satisfaction with communication, and productivity. *Psychological Reports*, 72(1), 171–7.

Morton, L. L., Kershner, J. R., & Siegel, L. S. (Winter, 1990). The potential for therapeutic applications of music on problems related to memory and attention. *Journal of Music Therapy*, 27(4), 195–208.

Nittono, H. (1997, June) Background instrumental music and serial recall. *Perceptual and Motor Skills*, 84(3 Pt 2), 1307–13.

Ransdell, S. E. & Gilroy, L. (2001). The effects of background music on word processed writing. *Computers in Human Behavior*, 17(2), 141–48.

10 Favorite Reggae Hits

Reggae originated in Jamaica and draws from Afro-American traditions. Listeners found it so soothing and grooving that it mainstreamed and flourished during the 1960s and 1970s (two famous artists are Bob Marley and Jimmy Cliff). It is strong in rhythm and percussion and rooted in political protest. Over time, traditional reggae "morphed" into a dancehall/DJ style of music, although it is still solidly Jamaican (you may have heard this style referred to as "ragga"). The songs on this list are among the best dance songs ever. Here are a few classics for your collection.

1. *Could You Be Loved* (Bob Marley)

2. *Money in My Pocket* (Dennis Brown)

3. *The Harder They Come* (Jimmy Cliff)

4. *Al Capone* (Prince Buster)

5. *Some Guys Have All the Luck* (Maxi Priest)

6. Selections from *Dance Hall Duo* (Frankie Paul)

7. *Pop Style* (Papa San) (combination of gospel and reggae)

8. Selections from *Stage One* (Sean Paul)

9. Selections from *No Holding Back* (Wayne Wonder)

10. Selections from *Good 2 Go* (Elephant Man)

7 Ways to Get Music (For Cheap or Free)

CD compilations are essential as a training tool—they spare you the hassle of interrupting a presentation in order to change CDs in the player. And customizing a CD is easier than ever, now that so many home computers come with CD burning software. Fee and subscription services available online have hundreds of thousands of titles to choose from, too.

1. Scour through your existing collections of music. You may already have many of the selections listed in this book.

2. Exchange CDs with other trainers or your friends.

3. Check out CDs from the public library's collection.

4. Buy compilation CDs (movie soundtrack CDs, for example, have lots of variety).

5. Shop at record stores that buy or exchange used CDs.

6. Buy specialty music from companies that specialize in training products.

7. Download music for cheap or free online. The following sites make it very easy.

    www.listen.com (Listen.com)
    www.napster.com (Napster)
    www.musicnow.com (MusicNow)
    www.itunes.com (Apple Computer's music store)
    www.walmart.com/musicdownloads (Wal-Mart)
    www.findanymusic.com
    www.ezmp3s.com/mydownloads.htm
    www.my-free-music.com/home.htm
    www.bresso.com

20 Fun Tunes for Children from Ages 3 to 6

Nothing brings a group of kids or adults together like a rousing chorus from a camp song. But playing music to young children is more than fun—their response to it can signal whether or not a child has hearing problems or doesn't understand the words. Finally, this age is the right time to expose children to how beautiful, exciting, and inspiring classical music can be.

For older learners, these selections evoke a playful state of consciousness. Use them for creativity, to accompany games, and to spur "outside of the box" thinking processes.

1. Songs by Gary Lapow

2. Songs by Hap Palmer

3. Songs by Red Grammer

4. German folk music

5. *The Scarf Dance* (Opus 37) (Cecile Chaminade)

6. Selections from *Whales and Nightingales* (Judy Collins)

7. Marches by John Philip Sousa

8. Selections from the soundtrack of *Jonathan Livingston Seagull*

9. *The Sorcerer's Apprentice* (appears on the *Fantasia soundtrack*) (Paul Dukas)

10. *Dance of the Hours* (appears on the *Fantasia* soundtrack) (Amilcare Ponchielli)

11. *Lincolnshire Posy* (Percy Grainger)

12. *Country Gardens* (traditional folk dance)

13. Selections from *Reggae for Kids* (Ras/Sanctuary)

14. Selections from *Greatest (Hits)* (The Go-Gos)

15. Disney movie soundtracks, like *The Lion King, Snow White, Dumbo,* and *Peter Pan*

16. Soundtrack to *The Wizard of Oz* (Harburg/Arlen)

17. Selections from *Joseph and the Amazing Technicolor Dreamcoat* (Rice/Webber)

18. *Peter and the Wolf* (Tchaikovsky)

19. *Tubby the Tuba* (George Kleinsinger)

20. *Mother Goose Suite* (Ravel)

16 Research Sources that Support the Use of Music in Teaching or Training

1. Anderson, C. A., Carnagey, N. L., & Eubanks, J. (2003, May). Exposure to violent media: The effects of songs with violent lyrics on aggressive thoughts and feelings. *Journal of Personality and Social Psychology*, 84(5), 960–71.

2. Anvari, S. H., Trainor, L. J., Woodside, J., & Levy, B. A. (2002, Oct). Relations among musical skills, phonological processing, and early reading ability in preschool children. *Journal of Experimental Child Psychology*, 83(2), 111–30.

3. Brouchard, R., Dufour, A., & Despres, O. (2004, Mar). Effect of musical expertise on visuospatial abilities: Evidence from reaction times and mental imagery. *Brain and Cognition*, 54(2), 103–9.

4. Burns, J. L., Labbe, E., Arke, B., Capeless, K., Cooksey, B., Steadman, A., & Gonzales, C. (2002). The effects of different types of music on perceived and physiological measures of stress. *Journal of Music Therapy*, 39(2), 101–16.

5. Chan, A. S., Ho, Y. C., & Cheung, M. C. (1998, Nov 12). Music training improves verbal memory. *Nature*, 396(6707), 128.

6. Fiske, Edward (Ed.) (1999). *Champions of Change: The Impact of the Arts on Learning*. Washington, DC: The Arts Education Partnership and the President's Committee on the Arts and Humanities.

7. Furnham, A. & Strbac, L. (2002, Feb 20). Music is as distracting as noise: The differential distraction of background music and noise on the cognitive test performance of introverts and extraverts. *Ergonomics*, 45(3), 203–17.

8. Gaser, C. & Schlaug, G. (2003, Oct 8). Brain structures differ between musicians and non-musicians. *Journal of Neuroscience*, 23(27), 9240–5.

9. Gregory, A., Worrall, L., & Sarge, A. (1996). The development of emotional responses to music in young children. *Motivation and Emotion*, 20(4), 341–8.

10. Gruhn, W., Galley, N., & Kluth, C. (2003, Nov). Do mental speed and musical abilities interact? *Annals of the New York Academy of Sciences*, 999, 485–96.

11. Lamb, S. J. & Gregory, A. H. (1993). The relationship between music and reading in beginning readers. *Educational Psychology*, 13(1), 19–26.

12. Rauscher, F. H., Shaw, G. L., & Ky, K. N. (1995, Feb 6). Listening to Mozart enhances spatial-temporal reasoning: Towards a neurophysiological basis. *Neuroscience Letters*, 185(1), 44–7.

13. Rauscher, F. H., Shaw, G. L., & Ky, K. N (1993, Oct 14). Music and spatial task performance. *Nature*, 365(6447), 611.

14. Rauscher, F. H., Shaw, G. L., Levine, L. J., Wright, E. L., Dennis, W. R., & Newcomb, R. L. (1997, Feb). Music training causes long-term enhancement of preschool children's spatial-temporal reasoning. *Neurological Research*, 19(1), 2–8.

15. Rohner, Stephen (1985). Cognitive-emotional response to music as a function of music and cognitive complexity. *Psychomusicology*, 5(1–2).

16. Yamamoto, T., Ohkuwa, T., Itoh, H., Kitoh, M., Terasawa, J., Tsuda, T., Kitagawa, S., & Sato, Y. (2003, July). Effects of pre-exercise listening to slow and fast rhythm music on supramaximal cycle performance and selected metabolic variables. *Archives of Physiology and Biochemistry*, 111(3), 211–4.

14 "Call-Back" Songs that Work like a Charm

For more than twenty years, I've used "call-back" songs as musical cues to let a class or group know it's time to get back to their seats. To establish the connection between the music and the action, play the song and then wander around the group saying, "It's our song—please find your seats!" After you've done this a few times, they will automatically link that tune to that behavior and start back to their seats without your prompting.

A call-back song usually has the following six qualities: 1) Its lyrics are clear and audible; 2) its lyrics are rated "G"; 3) it is in a major key (or has an upbeat sound); 4) it has a catchy melody or chorus; 5) it lasts between two and four minutes; and 6) it has a predictable and obvious conclusion (so everyone knows the exact moment it ends). All the songs on this list date back to the 1950s and 1960s but they are familiar to just about everyone. Any song that meets the above criteria, however, will serve this purpose.

1. *Rock Around the Clock* (Bill Haley and His Comets)

2. *Splish Splash* (Bobby Darin)

3. *Pretty Woman* (Roy Orbison)

4. *Get Back* (The Beatles)

5. *Do Wah Diddy Diddy* (Manfred Mann)

6. *Chantilly Lace* (The Big Bopper)

7. *Yakety Yak* (The Coasters)

8. *Walk Right In* (The Rooftop Singers)

9. *Shout* (The Isley Brothers)

10. *Rockin' Robin* (Bobby Day)

11. *Blue Moon* (The Marcels)

12. *Great Balls of Fire* (Jerry Lee Lewis)

13. *At the Hop* (Danny and the Juniors)

14. *Blue Suede Shoes* (Carl Perkins)

1 Legal Tip about Using Music: Get a License

Know the copyright laws! As a general rule, if your audience pays to hear you, you need to pay for a usage license. For example, if you are a K–12 teacher playing music in the classroom, you *don't* need a license. If you are a private tutor or a school principal playing music over the loudspeaker to the entire student body, you probably *do not* need a license. If you are a staff developer, administrator, or college-level teacher playing music for public consumption, you *definitely* need a license. Why? Because you're using an artist's work and benefiting financially from it. Fortunately, licenses really don't cost that much. Although rates vary, you can probably buy one for not much more than $100.

An annual "blanket license" allows you to play the music of any artist in the licensing agency's database (more than three million artists!) for cumulative audiences up to two thousand people a year. (A minimal per-person fee is usually charged after you reach the two thousand person maximum.) Such a license can be purchased from Broadcast Music, Inc. (BMI) or the American Society of Composers, Authors, and Publishers (ASCAP). Visit their Web sites, www.bmi.com/licensing and www.ascap.com/licensing, for more information.

7 Spectacular Introductions

Introduce speakers with some pomp and circumstance (although be sure to warn them ahead of time so they aren't completely rattled).

1. Theme song from *The Flintstones* (Curtin/Hanna & Barbera)

2. Theme from *Peter Gunn* (Henry Mancini)

3. *Hallelujah Chorus* from *Messiah* (Handel)

4. Theme from *The Pink Panther* (Henry Mancini)

5. Theme from *Star Wars* (John Williams)

6. *Hot, Hot, Hot* (Alphonsus Cassell)

7. Theme from the 1984 Olympics (John Williams)

5 Tips for Getting Started

You can make your presentations absolutely first-class by using music, but introduce this element one step at a time. Start with just one or two CDs and work your way up. I typically bring twenty-four CDs to a workshop; I know another trainer who brings two hundred! When I first started using music, I played just one song. After I got comfortable with this style of presenting, I added another, then another. These five tips are my words of wisdom for helping you make the transition a smooth process.

1. *Use music to solve your biggest problem first.* If your biggest issue during presentations is quieting down the audience, invest in a relaxing set of tunes. If you always struggle with infusing your audience with energy, get a set of exciting ones.

2. *Test out your equipment at home before using it at work.* Make sure that you have worked out all the bugs and quirks with your CD player and its remote control before you begin to speak. A little practice goes a long way and you'll seem much more like the professional your audience expects.

3. *Procure your music.* If you're good with computers, you can burn a custom CD of the tunes you want to use. If you're not able to burn your own CDs, there are plenty of compilations for sale, new and used. Even better, get an i-Pod and start working with it in your presentations. It's smaller, easier, and all digital!

4. *Take charge and be confident.* The more tentative you seem about playing music during instruction, the more your audience will question its inclusion. Choose carefully, then act with confidence.

5. *Forgive yourself.* We all make mistakes when we embark on something new. When they do happen, relax, acknowledge them, smile, and move on. Decide what to do next time to avoid the mistake and then stop worrying about it. Music is supposed to be fun for you, too!

About the Author

Eric Jensen is a former teacher and current member of the Society for Neuro-science and New York Academy of Sciences. He has taught students of all levels, from elementary school through university. In 1981, Jensen co-founded SuperCamp, the nation's first and largest brain-compatible learning program, now with more than 40,000 graduates. He has written *Brain-Based Learning*, *Arts with the Brain in Mind*, *Super Teaching*, *Tools for Engagement*, and eighteen other books on learning and the brain.

A leader in the brain-based movement, Jensen has made more than forty-five visits to neuroscience labs and interacts with countless neuroscientists. He was the founder of the **Learning Brain EXPO**. Jensen has trained more educators and presenters worldwide in this field than anyone else. He is deeply committed to making a positive, significant, lasting difference in the way we learn. Currently, Jensen does staff development, conference speaking, and in-depth trainings. To schedule him, call (858) 642-0400, x301, or send an e-mail to diane@jlcbrain.com.

Suggestions?

There is no way on earth that one person can keep up with all the music, remem-ber the latest tunes, or do justice to every artist. If an omission from any list really bugs you, write to me. I always welcome comments about your favorite artists, off-the-wall songs, and memorable tunes. If I accidentally assigned a song to the wrong artist, please let me know so I can correct it. If you have some really novel ideas about ways to use music in teaching or training, I'd love to hear those, too! I can be reached at eric@jlcbrain.com.